Fact Finders®

Mount RUSHMORE

MYTHS, Legends, and FACTS

by Jessica Gunderson

Consultant:
Melodie Andrews, PhD
Associate Professor of Early American History
Minnesota State University

CAPSTONE PRESS
a capstone imprint

Fact Finders Books are published by Capstone Press,
1710 Roe Crest Drive, North Mankato, Minnesota 56003.
www.capstonepub.com

Library of Congress Cataloging-in-Publication Data
Gunderson, Jessica.
  Mount Rushmore : myths, legends, and facts / by Jessica Gunderson.
      pages cm. — (Fact finders. Monumental history)
  Includes bibliographical references and index.
  Summary: "Explores the myths, facts, and legends associated with Mount
Rushmore"— Provided by publisher.
  ISBN 978-1-4914-0203-0 (library binding)
  ISBN 978-1-4914-0208-5 (pbk.)
  ISBN 978-1-4914-0212-2 (ebook pdf)
  1. Mount Rushmore National Memorial (S.D.)—Juvenile literature. I. Title.
  F657.R8G86 2015
  978.3'93—dc23   2014007007

Editorial Credits
Bobbie Nuytten, lead designer; Charmaine Whitman, production specialist

Developed and Produced by Focus Strategic Communications, Inc.
Adrianna Edwards: project manager; Ron Edwards: editor; Rob Scanlan: designer
and compositor; Karen Hunter: media researcher; Francine Geraci: copy editor and
proofreader; Wendy Scavuzzo: fact checker

Photo Credits
Alamy: Danita Delimont, 28, Pegaz, 7; Courtesy Red Cloud Indian School and
Marquette University, Holy Rosary Mission–Red Cloud Indian School Records,
#00416, 27; Crazy Horse Memorial, 22; Deborah Crowle Illustrations, 11; iStockphotos:
Joe Cicak, 17 (top left); Landov: DPA/Jerzy Dabrowski, 23; Library of Congress, cover
(right), 1 (right), 8, 13, 14 (bottom), 15, 17 (top right and bottom), 19, 26; National
Archives and Records Administration, 12; National Park Service, U.S. Department
of the Interior, 9; National Park Service: Mount Rushmore National Memorial,
cover (background), 5, 18, 20, 24, 25; Newscom: Stock Connection Worldwide/
Paul Horsted, 29; Shutterstock: Alex Pix, cover (bottom), back cover, 1 (bottom), 3,
James Steidl, 21; South Dakota State Historical Society, 6; South Dakota Tourism, 4;
Wikimedia, 14 (top), Jake DeGroot, 10

Design Elements by Shutterstock

Printed in the United States of America in Stevens Point, Wisconsin.
032014   008092WZF14

Table of Contents

Chapter ONE

BORGLUM'S VISION

The Black Hills of South Dakota are a place of legend and mystery. Thick pine forests make the hills look black, which is how they got their name. The Lakota Sioux called them *Páha Sápa*, or hills of black. Spires of needle-shaped granite pierce the sky.

The hills are rich in beauty. They also hold some of the largest man-made sculptures in the world. Four presidents look over the Black Hills to the plains beyond. The faces of George Washington, Thomas Jefferson, Theodore Roosevelt, and Abraham Lincoln are etched forever in stone.

the Black Hills of South Dakota

To many, Mount Rushmore is a symbol of democracy and freedom. But this stone shrine has a different message for others, such as American Indians. The granite faces in the South Dakota Black Hills hold many mysteries. Why was the monument created? Was it sculpted by a man who valued democracy, or did he have a secret agenda? What is held inside a hidden chamber behind the faces? Is Mount Rushmore on stolen land? Come closer. Explore the mysteries, myths, and legends of Mount Rushmore.

Every year nearly 3 million people visit Mount Rushmore. People come from all over the world to see the sight that stands as a symbol of the United States and its leaders.

The Birth of Mount Rushmore

Visitors to Mount Rushmore marvel at its enormous size and lifelike sculptures. Many wonder who designed and planned the monument. The credit usually goes to sculptor Gutzon Borglum. But the original idea wasn't his. So who were the people behind the vision?

In the early 1920s South Dakota historian Doane Robinson read about plans for the Stone Mountain monument in Georgia. He imagined a similar memorial in the Black Hills. He pictured large, dramatic carvings of western heroes such as Buffalo Bill Cody and Sioux Chief Red Cloud. He hoped that people would come from all over to see the sculptures.

Doane Robinson

STONE MOUNTAIN

Stone Mountain is home to the **Confederate** Memorial Carving. The huge carving shows three Confederate heroes— Jefferson Davis, Robert E. Lee, and Thomas "Stonewall" Jackson. Borglum was hired to work on the mountain but left before the project was completed.

Confederate: a person who supported the South during the Civil War

The Confederate Memorial Carving is at Stone Mountain in Georgia. The idea for the memorial was first thought of in 1916, but it was not finished until 1972.

Gutzon Borglum

Robinson contacted sculptor Gutzon Borglum, who had worked on Stone Mountain. Borglum accepted the project but dismissed Robinson's western heroes idea. He wanted a sculpture that would attract national attention. Gutzon saw the faces of U.S. presidents rising from the Black Hills.

Borglum was a world-famous sculptor who had trained in Paris. His bust of Abraham Lincoln was displayed in the White House. He designed the Stone Mountain monument in 1915. But Borglum also had a reputation for drama. While working on Stone Mountain, he argued often with the men in charge. His temper eventually got him fired from the job. He left, taking all his sketches and models with him so other sculptors couldn't copy them.

Gutzon Borglum

MEETING ON THE MOUNTAIN

The same year Borglum designed Stone Mountain, a controversial group met on top of the mountain—the **Ku Klux Klan**. Stone Mountain owner and Klan member, Samuel Venable, was at the meeting. This group helped fund the Stone Mountain carving.

Ku Klux Klan: a group that promotes hate against African-Americans, Catholics, Jews, immigrants, and other groups

Gutzon Borglum working on Stone Mountain

In 1925 Borglum traveled to South Dakota to scout locations for the sculpture. He brought his 12-year-old son Lincoln along. In those days the Black Hills were remote and rugged. Unpaved dirt roads and narrow paths weaved through the terrain. When Borglum saw the Needles formations, he quickly rejected them. He said he did not want to "make totem poles of these wonderful spires." He wanted something grander, higher, and more massive.

From the top of Harney Peak, the highest point in the Black Hills, Borglum spotted Mount Rushmore. The mountain's large granite mass, height, and southeast sun exposure was exactly what he was looking for. "Here is the place!" Borglum exclaimed. "American history shall march along that skyline."

Harney Peak

Mount Rushmore, Harney Peak, and the Needles locations

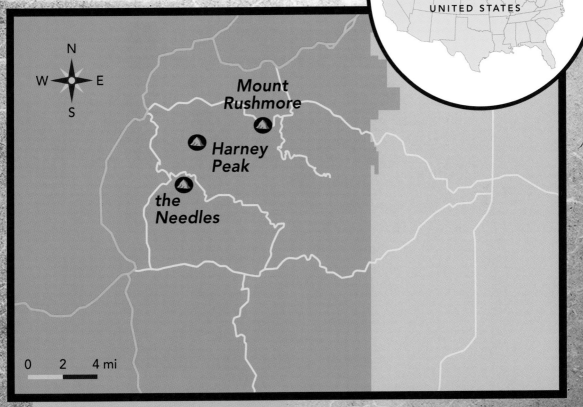

Mount Rushmore, Harney Peak, and the Needles are located in South Dakota.

AMERICAN INDIANS AND RUSHMORE

For centuries Indian tribes, such as the Arikara, Cheyenne, Crow, Pawnee, and Lakota Sioux, lived near the Black Hills. In the mid-1800s, settlers began moving west. Many American Indians resisted the **intrusion** upon their land and hunting grounds. In 1868 the Treaty of Fort Laramie created the Great Sioux Reservation, a large area that included the Black Hills. The land now officially belonged to the Lakota Sioux. But in the 1870s, whispers of gold spread across the country. The Black Hills were about to change forever.

the signing of the Treaty of Fort Laramie in 1868

intrusion: to enter some place without invitation or permission

The Black Hills Gold Rush began in 1874 after General George Armstrong Custer was ordered to explore the Black Hills. He wanted to find out if the stories about gold in the hills were true. He announced that he'd found "gold among the roots of the grass." Newspapers around the country published the report. Thousands of gold-hungry miners scurried to make **claims** on Black Hills land. The fact that the land belonged to the Sioux was unimportant to the gold seekers.

claim: a piece of land given to or taken by someone in order to be mined

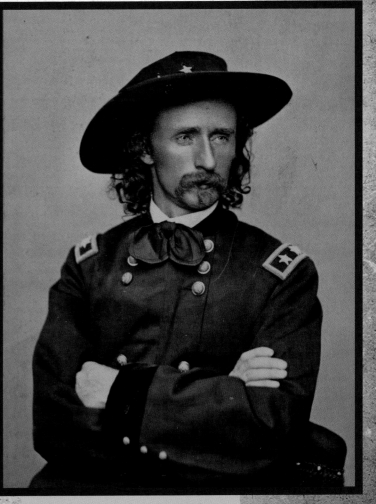

General George Armstrong Custer

Gold Rush

Wild, lawless towns, such as Deadwood, sprang up. The area drew stagecoach robbers, saloon halls, and fortune seekers. Legendary figures, such as Wild Bill Hickok and Calamity Jane, became a part of the Black Hills' history.

Despite these changes, the Sioux tried to maintain their traditional way of life. In 1875 the government tried to purchase the Black Hills, but the Lakota refused to sell. They considered the hills sacred. Battles broke out with the Sioux and Cheyenne tribes on one side and the U.S. Army on the other. This period was known as the Great Sioux War.

Wild Bill Hickok is a legendary figure in Black Hills history.

Calamity Jane's real name was Martha Jane Canary.

One of the most famous events of that war took place in June 1876, when the Sioux defeated General Custer at Little Big Horn. Custer was outnumbered, and the Sioux won easily. It was one of the only Sioux victories in a war to preserve their land and culture. The government saw the battle as a massacre. Government leaders wanted the Sioux to pay. In August they presented a treaty that required the Sioux to give up the Black Hills.

The only chiefs who could sign the new treaty were those who had not participated in the Great Sioux War. Anyone who refused to sign the treaty would be given no food. Their weapons and horses would be taken away. And the tribes would have to move anyway. Seeing no other alternative, the remaining Sioux chiefs signed the treaty.

Sitting Bull was one of the principal spiritual leaders of the Lakota during the Great Sioux War of 1876.

FACT In 1980 the Supreme Court ruled that the Black Hills were illegally taken from the Lakota Sioux. The Court required the government to pay the tribe $102 million for the land. The Sioux refused the money because they believed the Black Hills were taken illegally. They wanted the government to return their sacred land.

Chapter THREE

THE FOUR PRESIDENTS

George Washington, Thomas Jefferson, Theodore Roosevelt, and Abraham Lincoln are all known as great U.S. presidents. But why did Borglum select those four, and in that order and combination? Originally he planned to include just Washington, Lincoln, and Jefferson. Washington was the first U.S. president. He helped lay the foundation of American democracy. Jefferson, the third U.S. president, wrote the Declaration of Independence. He also encouraged **westward expansion** through the Louisiana Purchase, which doubled the size of the country. Lincoln, the nation's 16th president, fought to preserve the union and worked to abolish slavery.

Borglum began constructing a model for the sculpture, but soon realized there was room for one more face. He decided on Theodore Roosevelt, the 26th president and a man whom Borglum considered a friend. It was a controversial choice. Some argued that Roosevelt's presidency had been too recent. But Borglum prevailed and continued with his plan.

westward expansion: the idea of spreading the United States westward to encompass the continent

George Washington

Thomas Jefferson

Theodore Roosevelt

Abraham Lincoln

Chapter FOUR

SCULPTING THE MOUNTAIN

On October 4, 1927, President Calvin Coolidge handed Borglum six drill bits. Borglum used the bits to drill the first marks onto the granite face of Mount Rushmore. Although Borglum has been credited for Mount Rushmore's magnificence, he did not sculpt the faces himself. In fact, he did little of the hands-on drilling of the memorial. That job was left to the 400 workers he employed.

What Borglum did do was sculpt a model of the monument. He used portraits, photographs, and life masks to capture the faces of the presidents. On the model 1 inch equaled 1 foot on the mountain. Borglum then used a point system so workers could replicate the model upon the granite.

Hundreds of men worked on the monument.

The outside stone was too soft and fractured and needed to be removed. Sticks of dynamite blasted away many tons of this stone, exposing the hard granite beneath. Even then some of the granite was unsuitable for carving. Borglum changed his design nine times because of the rock's conditions. Jefferson was originally placed on Washington's right. After 18 months of carving, the crew hit faulty rock. Jefferson's head was blasted away and restarted on Washington's left. A crack in Jefferson's nose forced Borglum to move the head even farther to the left. Around 450,000 tons (408,233 metric tons) of rock were blasted away to create the monument.

BORGLUM'S SCALE MODEL

Borglum built a scale model to help him plan the sculptures. He measured the angles on his model using protractors and rulers. The measurements were then multiplied to match the scale of the mountain. A large, protractor-like tool on the mountain helped figure out how much rock to remove.

Gutzon Borglum's Model of Mt. Rushmore Memorial Washington, Jefferson, Roosevelt & Lincoln
—RISE STUDIO—

Around 90 percent of Mount Rushmore was carved with dynamite.

Construction Begins

During the 14-year construction, Mount Rushmore was alive with activity. Blasts of dynamite echoed throughout the hills. Shouts of workers and squeals of machinery filled the air. Wind, rain, and sometimes snow pummeled the mountain. Each morning the workers had to climb 760 steps to reach the mountaintop. The job was hard and dangerous. Workers were expected to swing from harnesses thousands of feet above the ground. Some, frightened by the extreme height of the mountain, left after just one day.

Despite the dangerous working conditions, no workers were killed. But one scary incident happened when five men were riding the **tramway** down the mountain. A cable pulley broke, and the tram sped out of control toward the bottom. One terrified worker jumped to the rocks below. He shattered an arm and his ribs. One of the men in the tram managed to wedge a piece of wood against the hoist wheel. That was enough to slow the descent. No one else was injured.

tramway: a transportation system for moving minerals or people; some are on the ground and some are in the air

Working on the tramway was difficult and dangerous.

20

According to local legend, the coffee break originated on Mount Rushmore. One cold morning the crew was taking a break and warming themselves with coffee. Borglum burst in the door and demanded to know what was going on. When they told him, Borglum turned to his handyman and said, "See to it that at 10 o'clock every morning we get some doughnuts and hot coffee up here!"

FACT The workers liked to have fun on the job. Their favorite prank was to loosen a new worker's safety cable and drop him a few feet to scare him.

Even some schoolchildren saved pennies to help fund the sculpture.

COST OF BUILDING THE MONUMENT

Mount Rushmore cost nearly $1 million to build, which is about $16 million in today's dollars. It was funded both with government money and private donations. The project barely got underway before the stock market crashed and the Great Depression began. There was no longer any money for construction. Progress on the monument stalled. Borglum personally went on fund-raising trips to convince Americans to donate.

Opposition

The massive project went ahead, but not everyone welcomed it. Some South Dakotans opposed the project. They thought a mountain sculpture would ruin the natural beauty of the Black Hills. Many American Indians saw Mount Rushmore as an insult. Built on sacred, stolen land, they felt Mount Rushmore and its **colossal** size represented white domination over their culture. Many Lakota Sioux still view the memorial as graffiti upon sacred ground. In 1929 Chief Henry Standing Bear imagined a sculpture that would honor his people.

colossal: extremely large

Chief Henry Standing Bear (right) and sculptor Korczak Ziolkowski

CRAZY HORSE MEMORIAL

Fifteen miles (24 kilometers) away from Mount Rushmore, another great sculpted mountain rises from the Black Hills. An answer to Mount Rushmore, the Lakota warrior Crazy Horse is being constructed for all to see. Sculptor Korczak Ziolkowski took on the project. In 1948 work on the monument began. The work continues to this day.

Crazy Horse is the world's largest mountain carving in progress. All four of the heads on Mount Rushmore could fit inside Crazy Horse's head. The statue is being built with Crazy Horse's left hand pointing to the distance. Legend says that he is answering the question, "Where are your lands now?" His answer? "My lands are where my dead lie buried."

Every year thousands of tourists visit Crazy Horse Memorial.

Chapter FIVE

MOUNT RUSHMORE TODAY

Many who gaze at Mount Rushmore see just the faces of the presidents. Not many realize that a forbidden, secret chamber is hidden behind those stony eyes. A small, treacherous path leads to a sealed **titanium** vault under a granite capstone. The entrance looks as though it belongs in ancient Egypt, not in a South Dakota mountain. Only a few photographs of the entrance exist. What could the monument be hiding?

Once again Borglum is at the mystery's center. Borglum had planned to make the monument even grander than it is today. His fear was that the reason for the monument would be lost. Future generations should know why Mount Rushmore was built.

titanium: a light, strong metal found in various minerals that is used to make steel

His next idea was a chamber drilled deep into the mountain. This Hall of Records would be visually inspiring. It would have a door of gold and glass and blue and gold walls. Inside would be bronze statues of historic figures, the original Constitution, and the Declaration of Independence. A written history of the nation, biographies of the presidents, and a biography of Borglum would be there too.

Borglum spent so much time on the Hall of Records that he abandoned the faces. The U.S. government ordered him to resume work on the monument. The chamber was left unfinished.

PLATES OF HISTORY

In 1998 the National Park Service fulfilled part of Borglum's dream. The written histories Borglum hoped to place in the Hall of Records were printed on 16 porcelain plates. The plates were sealed inside the Hall of Records to be preserved for decades to come.

the plaque at the entrance to the Hall of Records

MCMXCVIII

Completing Mount Rushmore

The presidential faces on the mountain look perfect. The truth is that they're unfinished. Borglum's original model has the presidents' bodies carved to the waist.

Borglum died unexpectedly in 1941, 14 years after the project started. His son Lincoln took over, but World War II (1939–1945) made future funding impossible. Lincoln Borglum focused on finishing what he could—the heads. Washington's collar and the beginning of Lincoln's knuckles were completed too.

Visitors often wonder if the mountain could hold more faces. They also ask if another president could be added in the future. The idea has been explored. In 1937 two senators proposed adding the face of women's rights leader Susan B. Anthony. The idea fell through because of lack of funding. In recent years Congress has discussed adding former president Ronald Reagan's likeness. The idea has never gained much support.

Susan B. Anthony played an important role in the women's rights movement.

BEN BLACK ELK

One man was often called the "fifth face on the mountain." For 27 years Ben Black Elk greeted visitors to Mount Rushmore. The son of a Lakota holy man, Ben dressed in traditional clothing and shared stories of Lakota culture. Thousands of tourists posed with him for pictures between the 1950s and 1970s. Ben's photograph graced many state and national newspapers and magazines. Today the Ben Black Elk Award is given to a person who has made contributions to South Dakota's tourism industry.

Ben Black Elk

National Treasure

Mount Rushmore has become part of Hollywood legend. It was included in movies such as *North by Northwest* and *National Treasure: Book of Secrets*. Various films have portrayed the monument as a secret hideout, a chase scene location, or the entrance to a city of gold. Other movies replace the presidential faces with faces of movie characters.

While there is no city of gold or criminal hideouts, Mount Rushmore itself is a national treasure. It has been a gathering place for the Lakota Sioux. Today visitors can learn more about Lakota history at Heritage Village, an exhibit near the monument. Lakota Sioux practice traditional arts and explain American Indian history and Lakota culture to tourists.

Geologists estimate that the sculpture will erode only 1 inch (2.5 centimeters) every 10,000 years, so the memorial to these great presidents will live on for future generations who may one day wonder about the mysteries it holds.

visitors today at Mount Rushmore

PRESERVING THE MONUMENT

The natural rock of Mount Rushmore contains cracks and **fissures**. Every fall National Park Service staff apply a sealant to any cracks. Large cracks are patched with Kevlar material, which is the same stuff used in body armor. This keeps ice and snow out of the cracks and prevents splitting or other damage.

fissure: a split or crack, especially in rock or stone

maintenance work on Mount Rushmore

GLOSSARY

claim (KLAYM)—a piece of land given to or taken by someone in order to be mined

colossal (kuh-LAH-suhl)—extremely large

Confederate (kuhn-FE-dur-uht)—a person who supported the South during the Civil War

fissure (FISH-ure)—a split or crack, especially in rock or stone

intrusion (in-TROO-zhuhn)—to enter some place without invitation or permission

Ku Klux Klan (KOO KLUHX KLAN)—a group that promotes hate against African-Americans, Catholics, Jews, immigrants, and other groups

titanium (tahy-TEY-nee-uhm)—a light, strong metal found in various minerals that is used to make steel

tramway (TRAM-way)—transportation system for moving minerals or people; some are on the ground and some are in the air

westward expansion (WEST-wurd ik-SPAN-shuhn)—the idea of spreading the United States westward to encompass the continent

READ MORE

Goldsworthy, Kaite. *Mount Rushmore*. American Icons. New York: AV2 by Weigl, 2013.

O'Mara, Mary. *Visit Mount Rushmore*. Landmarks of Liberty. New York: Gareth Stevens Publishing, 2012.

Thomas, William David. *Mount Rushmore*. Symbols of American Freedom. New York: Chelsea Clubhouse, 2009.

CRITICAL THINKING USING THE COMMON CORE

1. The Sioux have never wanted Mount Rushmore to be used as a public monument. Why? What are three things the Lakota Sioux have done to show how upset they were? Use details and evidence from the text to answer the questions. (Key Ideas and Details)

2. Why did Borglum pick Washington, Lincoln, Jefferson, and Roosevelt for the sculptures? Use details from the text to explain why he believed each president was important. (Key Ideas and Details)

3. Look at the photo of the monument on page 5. Then look at the photo of Borglum's model on page 19. Next read the first paragraph on page 26. Use this information to answer the question: What parts of Borglum's plan have actually been sculpted on Mount Rushmore? Explain where you found each detail you put in your answer. (Integration of Knowledge and Ideas; Key Ideas and Details)

INTERNET SITES

FactHound offers a safe, fun way to find Internet sites related to this book. All of the sites on FactHound have been researched by our staff.

Here's all you do:

Visit *www.facthound.com*

Type in this code: 9781491402030

 Check out projects, games, and lots more at
www.capstonekids.com

INDEX